100 FACTS ABOUT AUSTRALIA

Exploring the Wonders of the Land Down Under

Welcome to a captivating journey through the Land Down Under, a place of incredible beauty and cultural richness. "100 Facts About Australia" is your gateway to an exploration of the diverse landscapes, unique wildlife, vibrant cultures, and fascinating histories that define this remarkable continent.

Join us as we embark on a voyage through Australia's charm, grandeur, and undeniable significance. From ancient wonders to modern marvels, from the iconic landmarks to the hidden treasures, this book is a tribute to the essence of Australia. Whether you're a traveler, history buff, or simply curious about the world, our journey through these 100 facts promises to inform, inspire, and ignite your passion for the wonders of Australia.

Discover the stories of resilience, creativity, and natural splendor that make Australia a land like no other. Each fact you encounter will unveil a different facet of this extraordinary place. So, turn the page, and let the adventure begin.

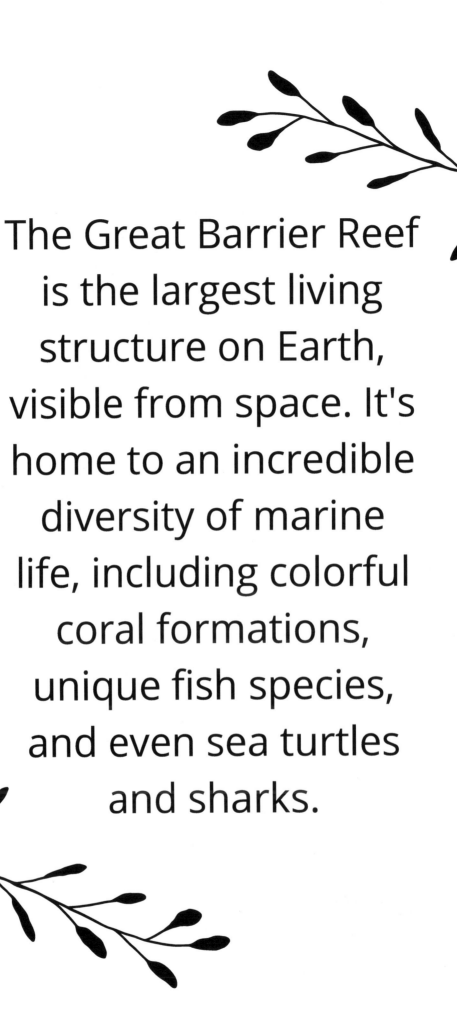

The Great Barrier Reef is the largest living structure on Earth, visible from space. It's home to an incredible diversity of marine life, including colorful coral formations, unique fish species, and even sea turtles and sharks.

Uluru, also known as Ayers Rock, is a massive sandstone formation in the Australian Outback. Its color changes dramatically at sunrise and sunset due to the angle of the sun's rays, ranging from red to purple to orange.

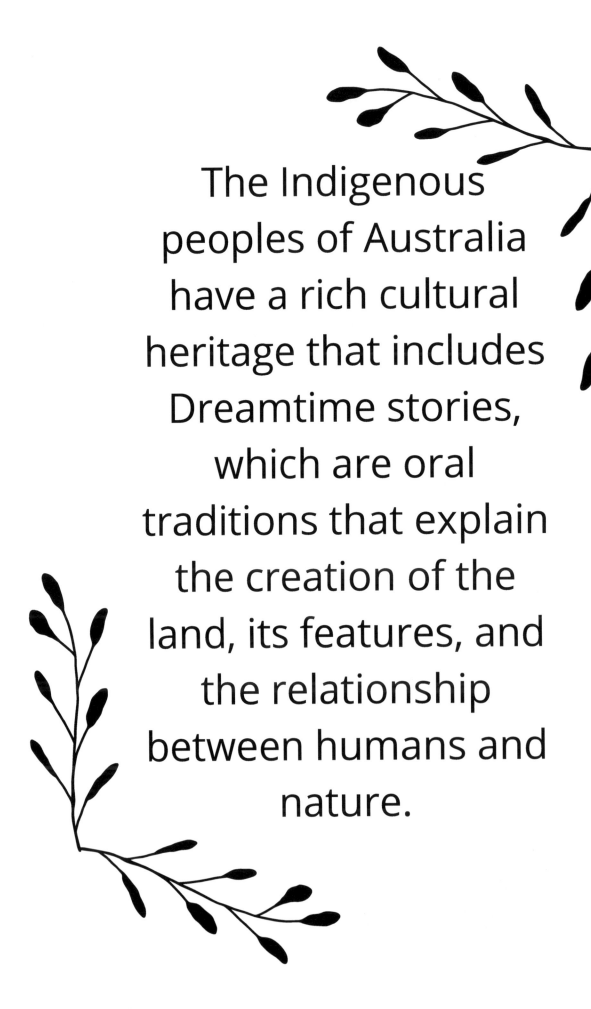

The Indigenous peoples of Australia have a rich cultural heritage that includes Dreamtime stories, which are oral traditions that explain the creation of the land, its features, and the relationship between humans and nature.

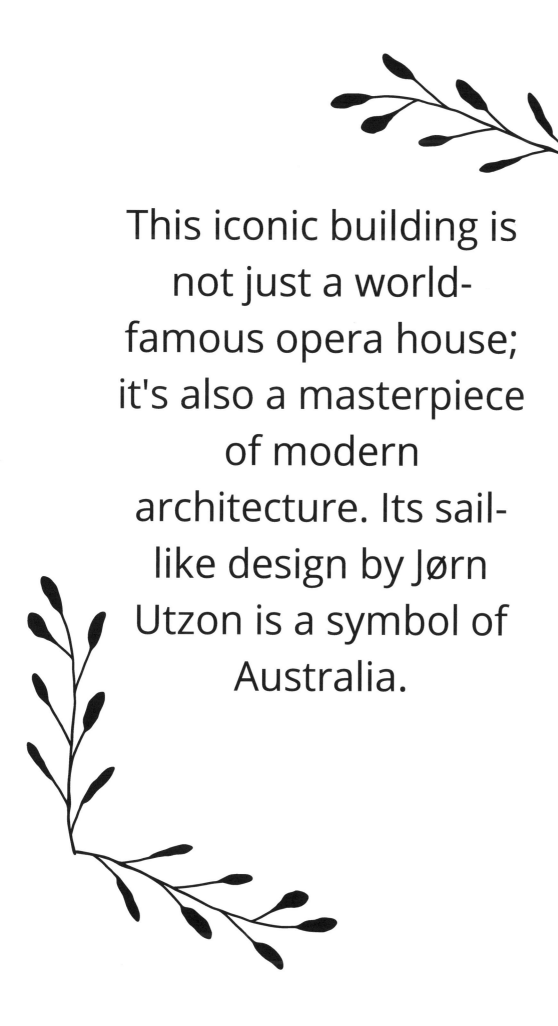

This iconic building is not just a world-famous opera house; it's also a masterpiece of modern architecture. Its sail-like design by Jørn Utzon is a symbol of Australia.

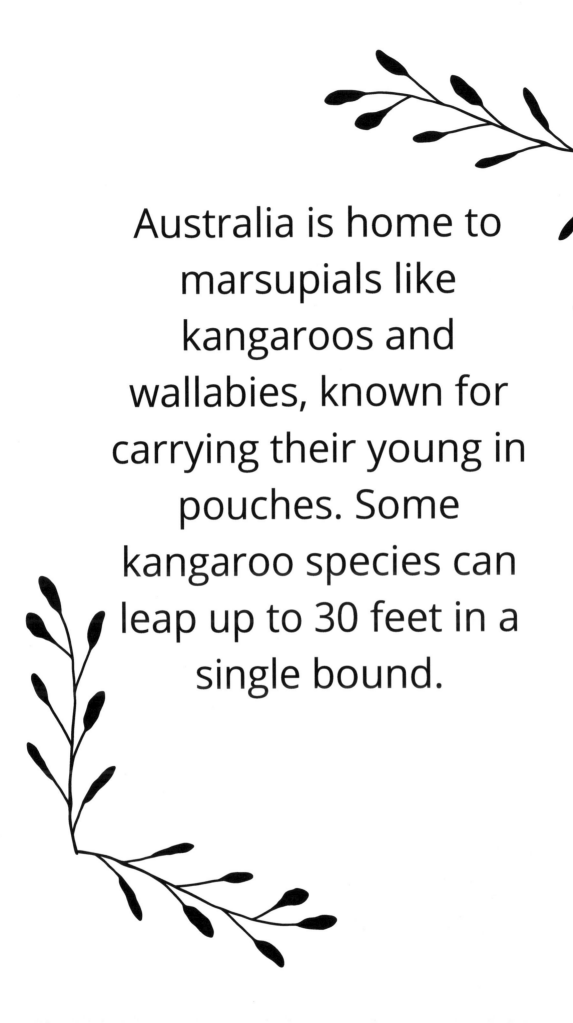

Australia is home to marsupials like kangaroos and wallabies, known for carrying their young in pouches. Some kangaroo species can leap up to 30 feet in a single bound.

Located in
Queensland, this is
the oldest tropical
rainforest in the
world, dating back
over 135 million years.
It's a UNESCO World
Heritage site.

Boomerangs, originally used by Indigenous Australians for hunting, are returning tools that can be thrown in such a way that they come back to the thrower.

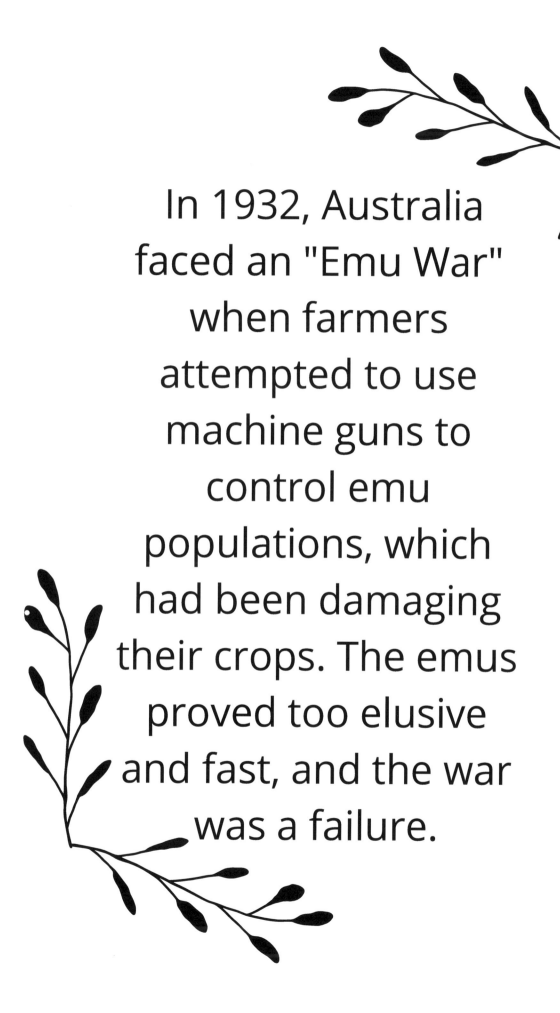

In 1932, Australia faced an "Emu War" when farmers attempted to use machine guns to control emu populations, which had been damaging their crops. The emus proved too elusive and fast, and the war was a failure.

These carnivorous marsupials are known for their fierce temperament and spine-chilling screeches. They're found only on the island of Tasmania.

Lake Hillier, located on Middle Island in Western Australia, is a bright pink lake due to a unique combination of microorganisms and high salinity.

Home to the Bungle Bungle Range, these unique striped sandstone domes are a geological marvel and a UNESCO World Heritage site.

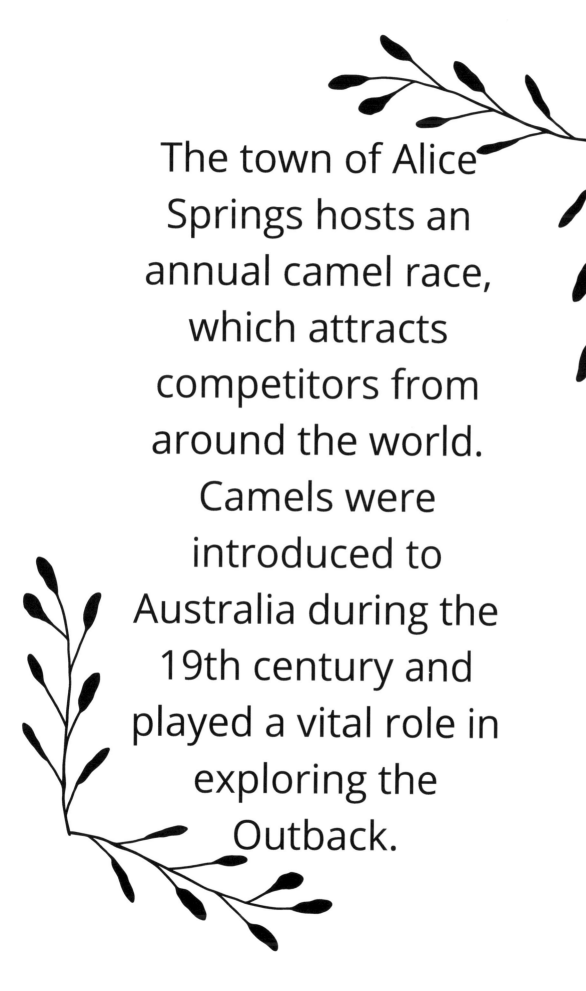

The town of Alice Springs hosts an annual camel race, which attracts competitors from around the world. Camels were introduced to Australia during the 19th century and played a vital role in exploring the Outback.

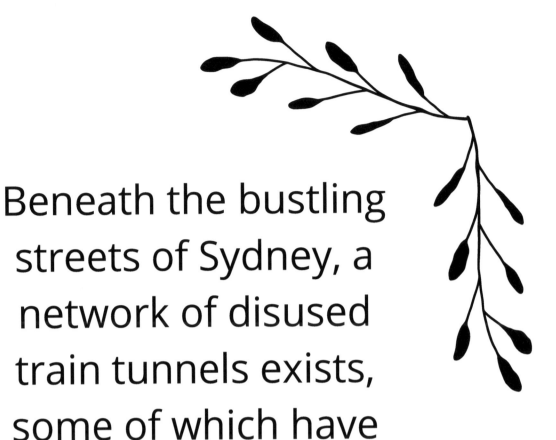

Beneath the bustling streets of Sydney, a network of disused train tunnels exists, some of which have been turned into vibrant street art galleries.

A natural phenomenon that occurs in Broome, Western Australia, where the rising full moon reflects on tidal mudflats, creating a beautiful optical illusion.

This park is known for its stunning Red Rock Gorge and boasts unique birdlife, including the rare squatter pigeon.

Kangaroo Island is home to the purest strain of Ligurian bees in the world, and it's renowned for its honey production.

The name "Nullarbor" is derived from Latin and means "no trees." This vast arid expanse is one of the largest limestone karst landscapes in the world.

These ancient mountains in Western Australia host unique flora, including the rare Banksia grandis, known for its massive flower spikes.

Australia's Simpson Desert contains the world's longest parallel sand dunes, creating a breathtaking and surreal landscape.

Located in Nambung National Park, these eerie limestone formations create an otherworldly lunar landscape.

This challenging sailing race, held annually on Boxing Day, covers over 1,000 kilometers and is considered one of the world's most challenging yacht races.

Coober Pedy: The Opal Capital: Known as the "opal capital of the world," this unique Australian town is famous for its underground homes and businesses to escape the scorching heat.

Stretching over 5,600 kilometers, this fence was built to keep dingoes (wild dogs) away from fertile land and protect livestock.

Dingoes are unique to Australia and play a crucial role in the country's ecosystems. They are believed to have been introduced around 4,000 years ago.

The Hazards Mountain Range: Located in Freycinet National Park, this range offers dramatic granite peaks, pristine beaches, and incredible views.

The Blue Mountains:
Just outside Sydney,
this World Heritage-
listed area is known
for its stunning blue-
tinged eucalyptus
forests, deep gorges,
and unique rock
formations.

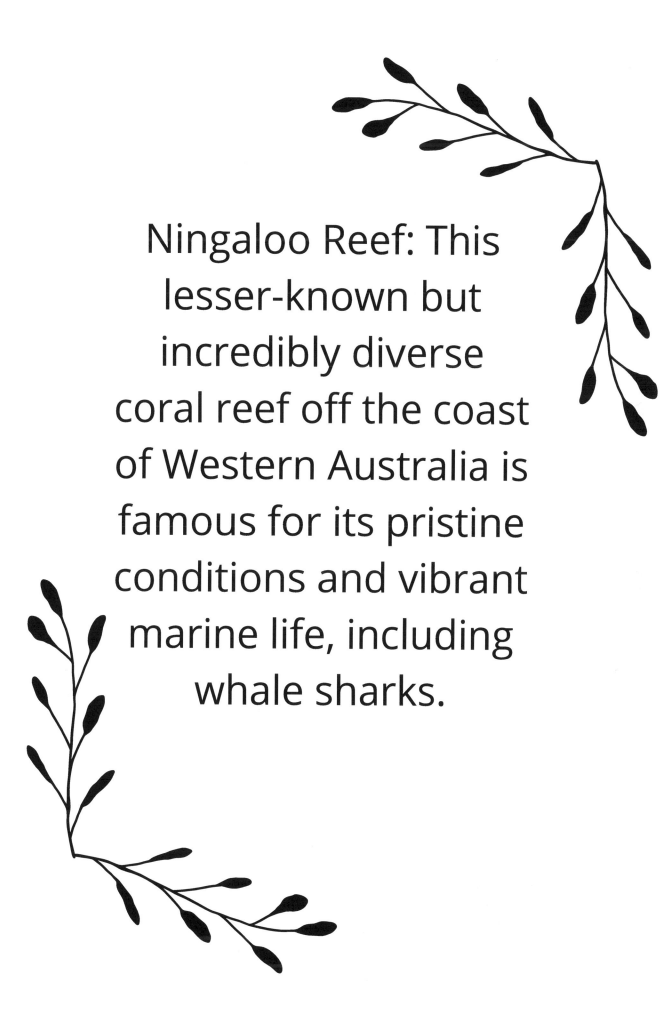

Ningaloo Reef: This lesser-known but incredibly diverse coral reef off the coast of Western Australia is famous for its pristine conditions and vibrant marine life, including whale sharks.

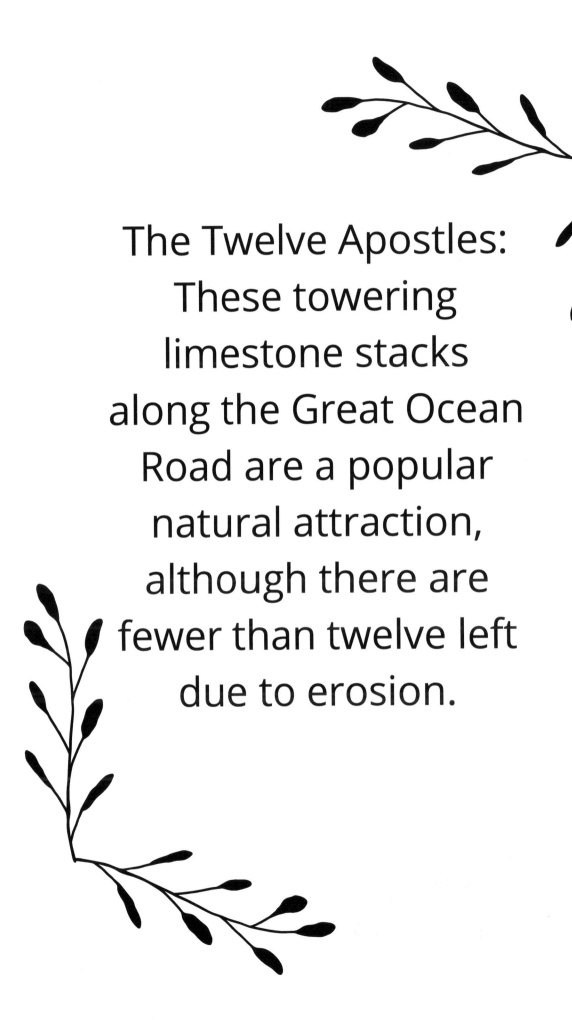

The Twelve Apostles: These towering limestone stacks along the Great Ocean Road are a popular natural attraction, although there are fewer than twelve left due to erosion.

The Royal Flying
Doctor Service:
Established in 1928,
this service provides
essential medical care
to remote outback
communities via
aircraft.

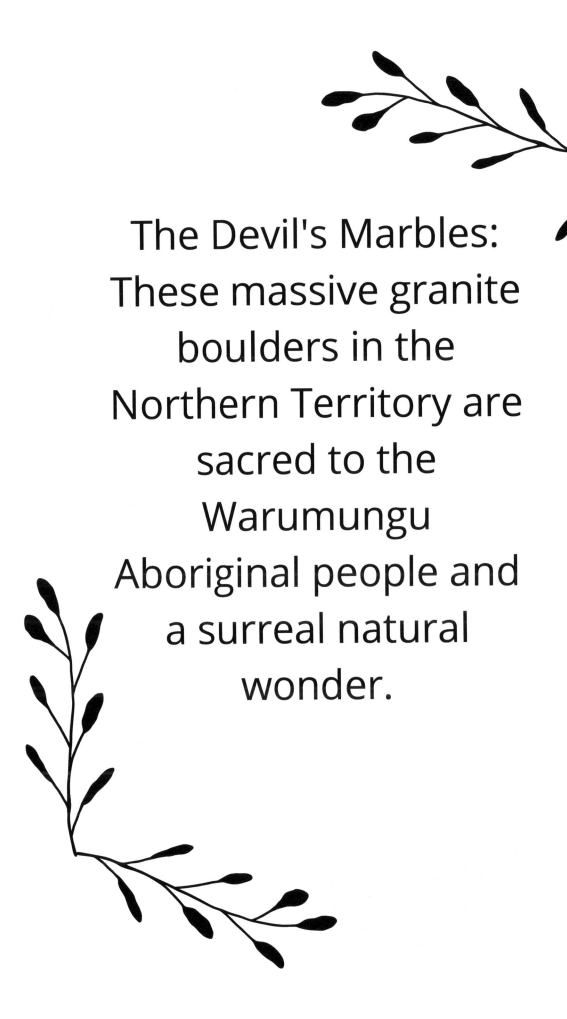

The Devil's Marbles:
These massive granite
boulders in the
Northern Territory are
sacred to the
Warumungu
Aboriginal people and
a surreal natural
wonder.

Straddling the borders of New South Wales and Victoria, the Australian Alps are not only a skiing destination but also home to unique flora and fauna.

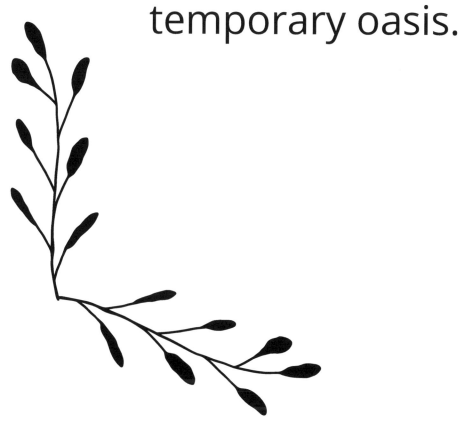

Lake Eyre: The largest salt lake in Australia, it's often dry but can fill with water during rare floods, transforming into a temporary oasis.

The Australian Magpie: This native bird, known for its melodious singing and striking black and white plumage, is unrelated to European magpies.

The Great Ocean Road: One of the world's most scenic drives, it hugs the Victorian coastline and offers breathtaking views of rugged cliffs and the Southern Ocean.

The Murray-Darling Basin: This vast river system covers one-seventh of Australia's landmass and is crucial for agriculture and biodiversity.

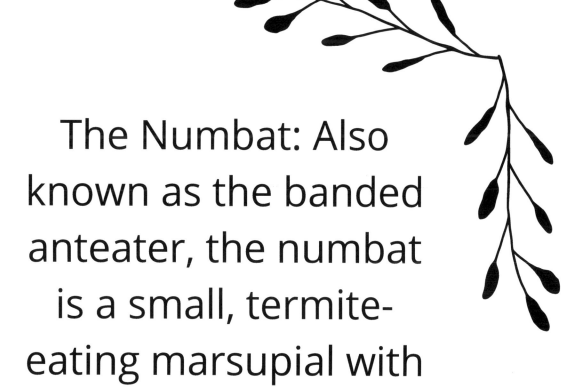

The Numbat: Also known as the banded anteater, the numbat is a small, termite-eating marsupial with striking orange markings.

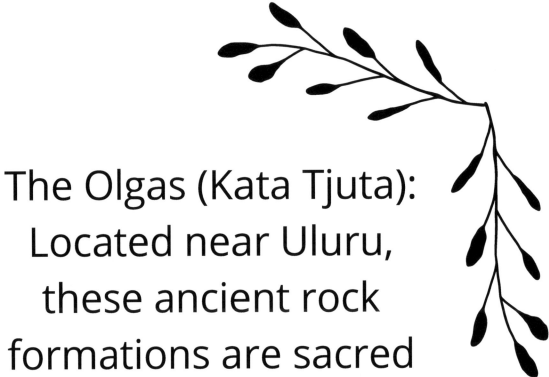

The Olgas (Kata Tjuta): Located near Uluru, these ancient rock formations are sacred to the Anangu people and offer awe-inspiring hikes.

The Green and Golden Bell Frog: This vibrant green and gold amphibian is native to Eastern Australia and is endangered due to habitat loss.

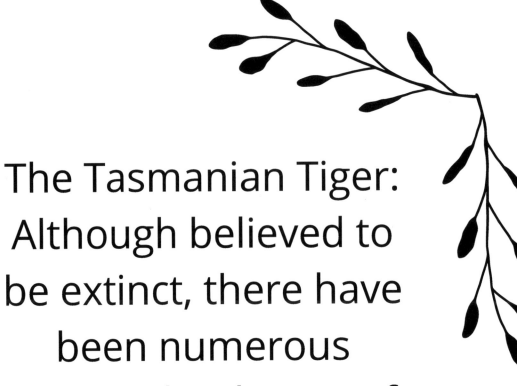

The Tasmanian Tiger:
Although believed to
be extinct, there have
been numerous
reported sightings of
this elusive marsupial.

The MacDonnell
Ranges: These ancient
mountain ranges in
the Northern Territory
are home to stunning
gorges, indigenous art
sites, and unique
wildlife.

The Flying Foxes: Australia is home to various species of flying foxes, which are large fruit bats known for their important role in pollination and seed dispersal.

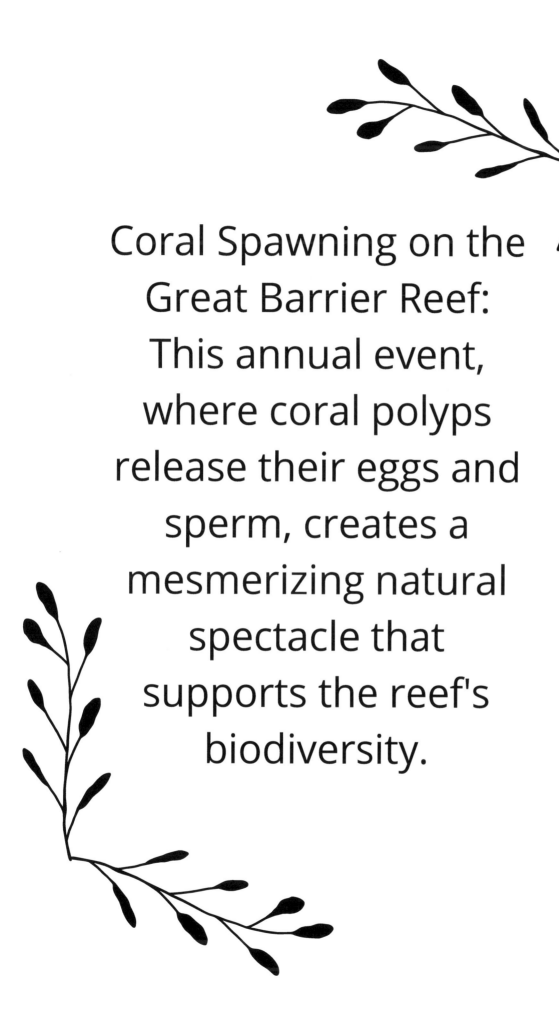

Coral Spawning on the Great Barrier Reef: This annual event, where coral polyps release their eggs and sperm, creates a mesmerizing natural spectacle that supports the reef's biodiversity.

The Lava Tubes of
Undara: Located in
North Queensland,
Undara's lava tubes
are the longest known
lava tube system on
Earth.

The Tasmanian Devil's Remarkable Bite: The Tasmanian Devil has one of the strongest bites per unit body mass of any living mammal.

The Rainbow Serpent:
In Indigenous
Australian mythology,
the Rainbow Serpent
is a significant cultural
symbol representing
the Dreamtime and
creation.

Fraser Island: The Largest Sand Island: Fraser Island, off the coast of Queensland, is the world's largest sand island, known for its pristine beaches and unique ecosystems.

The Australian Alps
Walking Track:
Stretching over 650
kilometers, this track
is a challenging hiking
adventure that passes
through alpine
landscapes.

The Pardalote Birds: These tiny, colorful birds are among the smallest in Australia and are known for their distinctive calls and burrow-nesting habits.

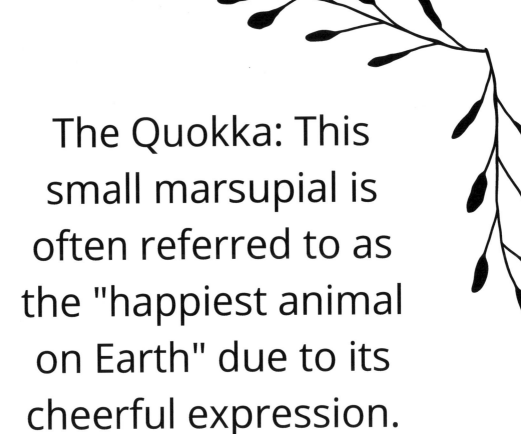

The Quokka: This small marsupial is often referred to as the "happiest animal on Earth" due to its cheerful expression.

The Ghost Mushroom:
This bioluminescent
fungus is native to
Australia and is found
in certain forests,
creating an
enchanting glow at
night.

The Kimberley's Horizontal Falls: A natural wonder, these tidal waterfalls are created by powerful tidal currents squeezing through narrow coastal gorges.

The Aurora Australis:
Also known as the
Southern Lights, this
natural light display is
visible from some
parts of Australia,
creating a stunning
celestial spectacle.

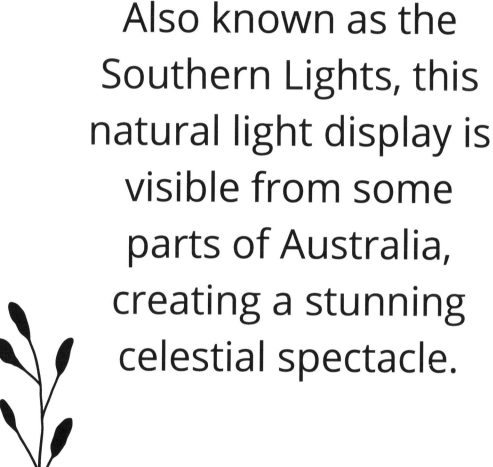

The Southern Right Whale: These massive whales migrate along the Australian coast, where they can often be spotted breaching and playing.

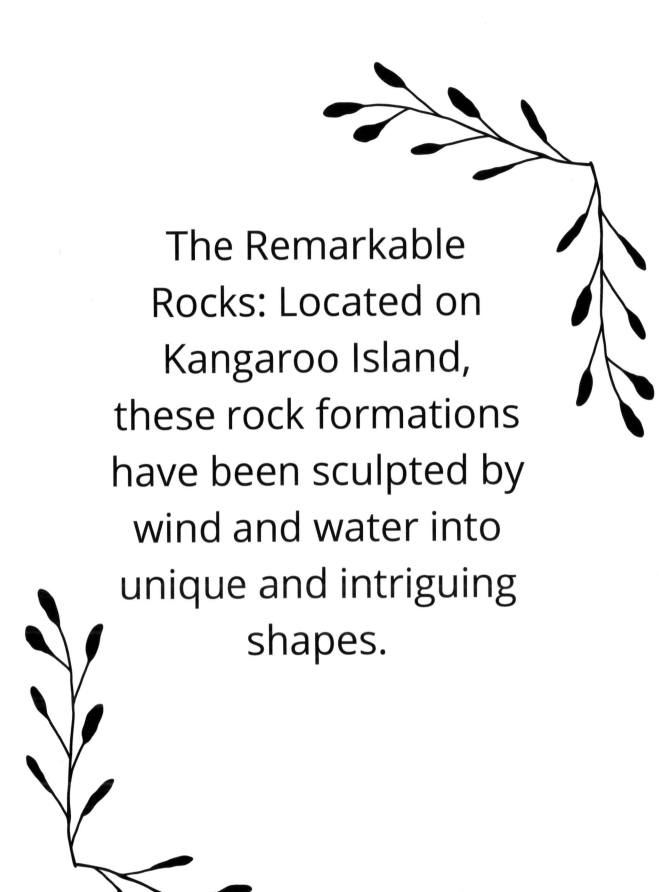

The Remarkable Rocks: Located on Kangaroo Island, these rock formations have been sculpted by wind and water into unique and intriguing shapes.

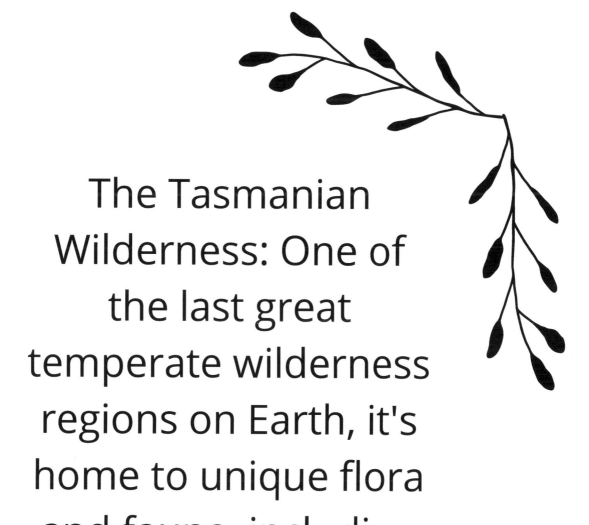

The Tasmanian
Wilderness: One of
the last great
temperate wilderness
regions on Earth, it's
home to unique flora
and fauna, including
the Tasmanian devil.

The Aboriginal Art of Papunya: This community in the Northern Territory is known for its role in the Western Desert art movement, with paintings telling stories of the Dreamtime.

The Cassowary: This flightless bird is one of the heaviest and most dangerous birds in the world, known for its striking blue skin and helmet-like casque.

The Tree Kangaroo:
Native to the
rainforests of
Northern Queensland,
the tree kangaroo is
an arboreal marsupial
that's adapted to life
in the treetops.

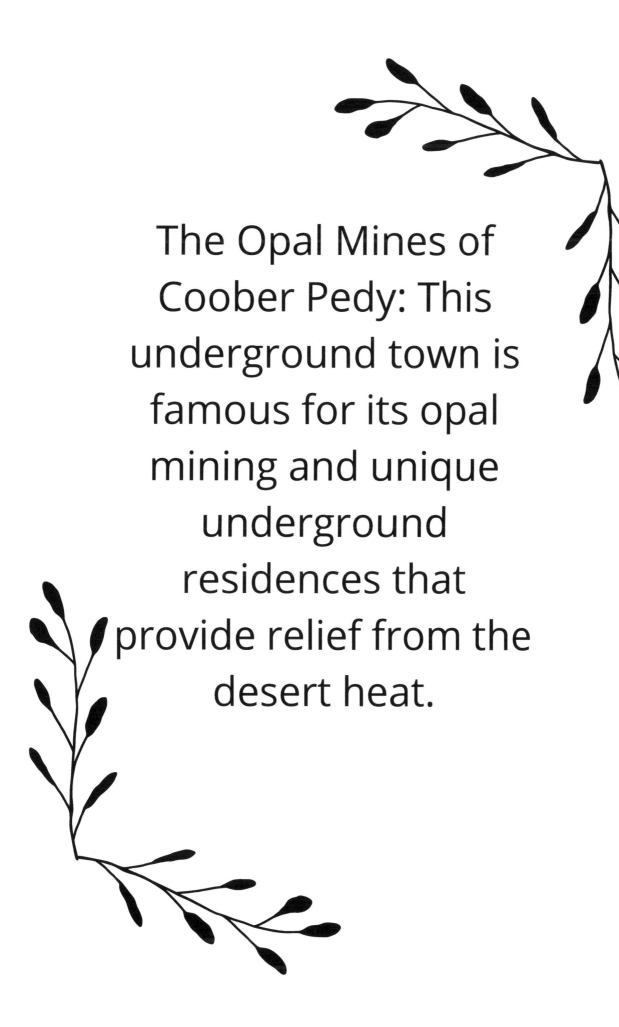

The Opal Mines of Coober Pedy: This underground town is famous for its opal mining and unique underground residences that provide relief from the desert heat.

The Overlanders: Early Australian pioneers known as "Overlanders" drove cattle vast distances to market, facing harsh conditions and challenges.

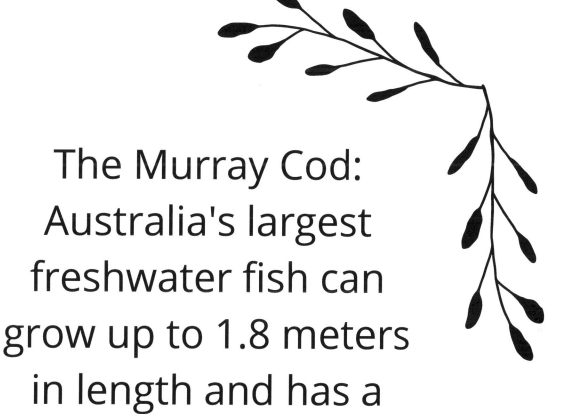

The Murray Cod:
Australia's largest
freshwater fish can
grow up to 1.8 meters
in length and has a
unique appearance
with mottled green
and yellow skin.

The White-Throated Treecreeper: This small bird is known for its distinctive call and unique habit of descending trees headfirst.

The Bungle Bungle Range: These distinctive striped sandstone domes in Purnululu National Park are a geological marvel and a UNESCO World Heritage site.

The Aurora Australis Ship: An icebreaker vessel that supports scientific research in Antarctica, showcasing Australia's commitment to understanding this frozen continent.

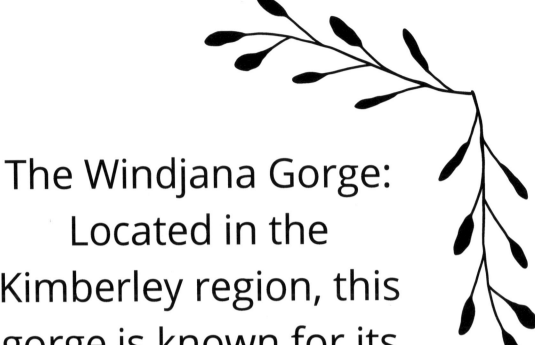

The Windjana Gorge:
Located in the
Kimberley region, this
gorge is known for its
towering cliffs and
fossils embedded in
its ancient limestone.

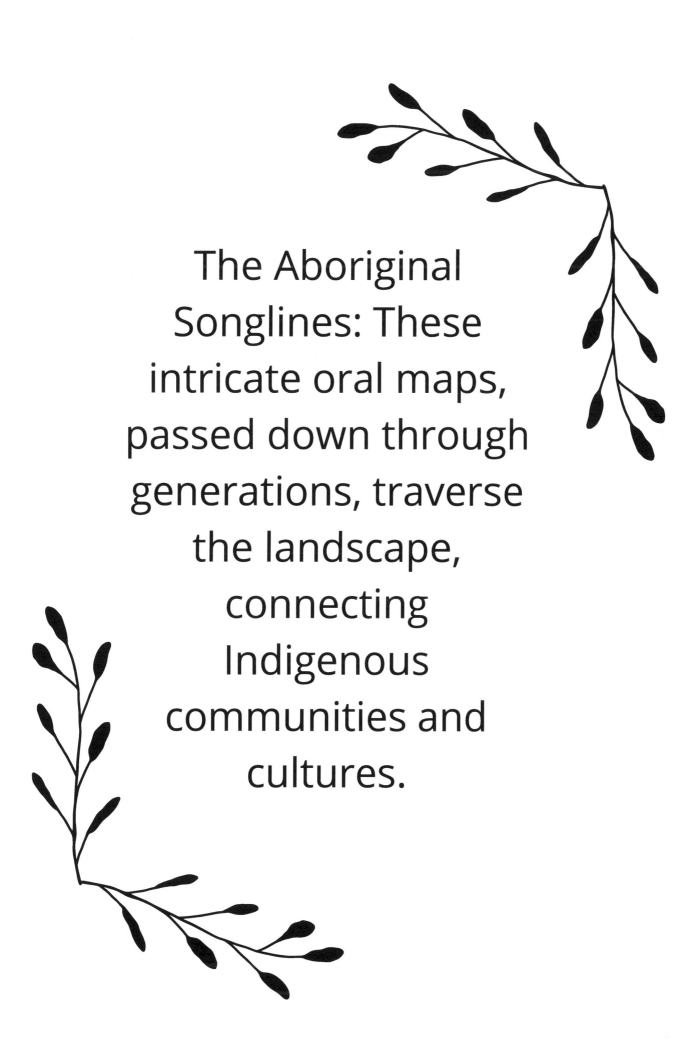

The Aboriginal Songlines: These intricate oral maps, passed down through generations, traverse the landscape, connecting Indigenous communities and cultures.

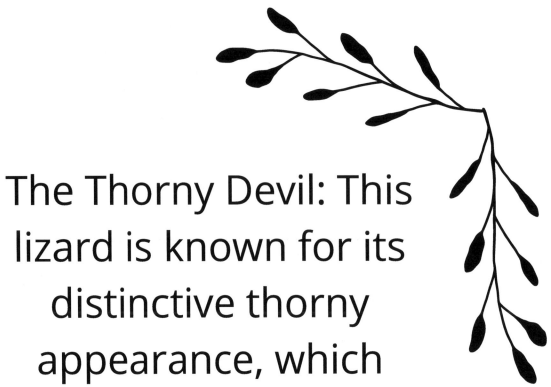

The Thorny Devil: This lizard is known for its distinctive thorny appearance, which helps it regulate its body temperature in the harsh Australian desert.

The Glow-in-the-Dark Fungi: Australia is home to various bioluminescent fungi, which can create an otherworldly glow in the dark.

The Longest Fence in the World: Stretching over 5,600 kilometers, the Dingo Fence is one of the longest structures built by humans.

The Perth Mint: This iconic institution is renowned for producing some of the world's most valuable coins and bullion.

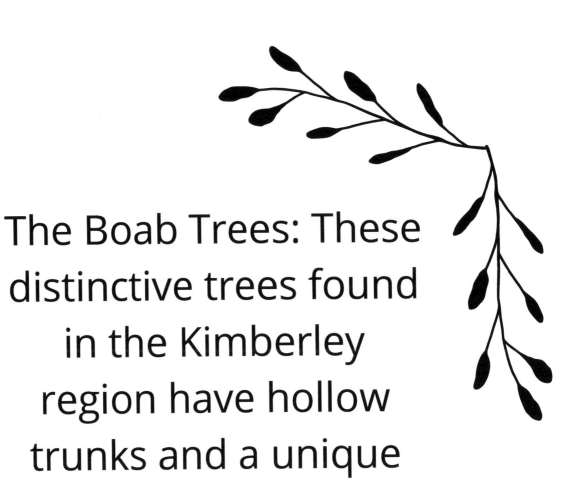

The Boab Trees: These distinctive trees found in the Kimberley region have hollow trunks and a unique appearance.

The Australian
Lyrebird: Renowned
for its remarkable
ability to mimic
sounds, the lyrebird
can imitate the calls of
other birds, cameras,
and even chainsaws.

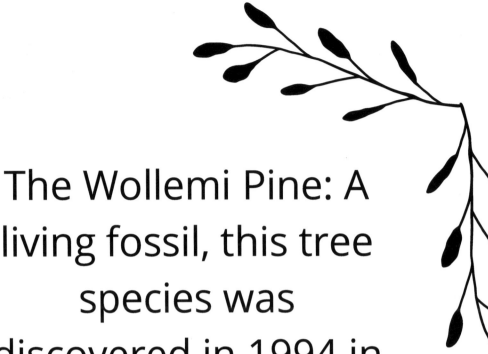

The Wollemi Pine: A living fossil, this tree species was discovered in 1994 in a remote canyon in Wollemi National Park.

The Queen's Land:
Australia is the only
continent entirely in
the Southern
Hemisphere and is
often referred to as
"the Queen's Land."

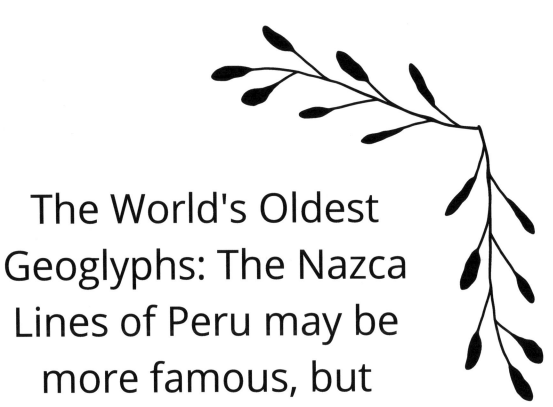

The World's Oldest
Geoglyphs: The Nazca
Lines of Peru may be
more famous, but
Australia's Marree
Man is one of the
largest

Oceania's Highest Mountain: Puncak Jaya in Papua New Guinea is Oceania's highest peak.

Vivid Sydney: An annual festival illuminating Sydney's landmarks with mesmerizing light displays.

Avalon Airshow: The Australian International Airshow showcases military and civilian aircraft.

Bungy Jumping: AJ Hackett introduced bungy jumping to the world, starting in New Zealand and then in Australia.

Dinosaur Footprints:
In the Kimberley
region, you can find
dinosaur footprints
dating back millions of
years, preserved in
the rock.

Crocodile Population: Australia is home to both saltwater and freshwater crocodiles, with the former being one of the largest reptiles on Earth.

Tasmanian Tiger Sightings: Despite being declared extinct, there are occasional reported sightings of the elusive Tasmanian tiger, or thylacine.

Bush Medicine:
Indigenous
communities in
Australia have a
wealth of traditional
bush medicines
derived from native
plants.

The World's Biggest Sundial: The Singleton Sundial in New South Wales is considered the world's largest sundial.

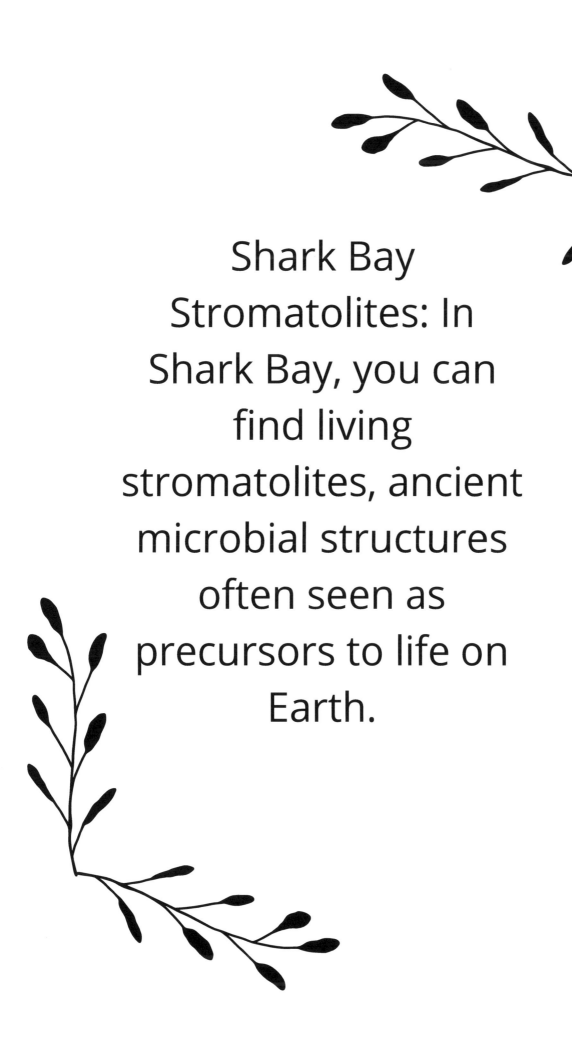

Shark Bay Stromatolites: In Shark Bay, you can find living stromatolites, ancient microbial structures often seen as precursors to life on Earth.

Brisbane's Lone Pine Koala Sanctuary: It's the world's first and largest koala sanctuary, established in 1927.

World's Largest Rock:
Mount Augustus in
Western Australia is
larger than Uluru,
often called the
world's largest rock.

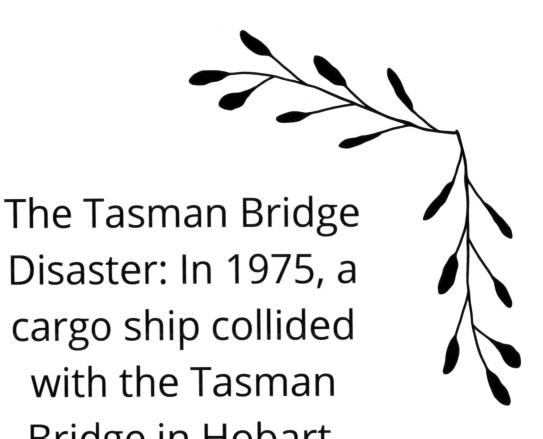

The Tasman Bridge Disaster: In 1975, a cargo ship collided with the Tasman Bridge in Hobart, Tasmania, causing a section of the bridge to collapse.

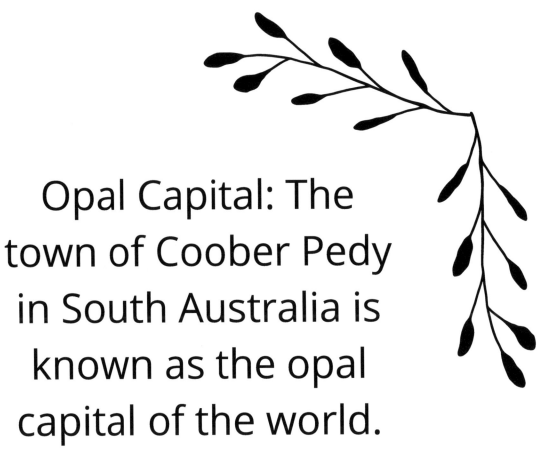

Opal Capital: The town of Coober Pedy in South Australia is known as the opal capital of the world.

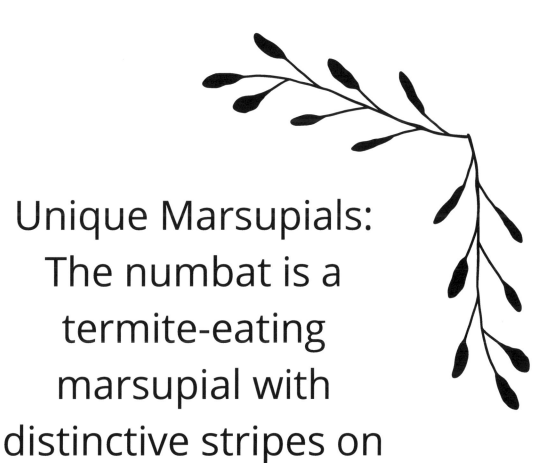

Unique Marsupials:
The numbat is a
termite-eating
marsupial with
distinctive stripes on
its back.

Qantas: Spirit of Australia: Qantas, Australia's national airline, is one of the world's oldest and was founded in 1920.

Inland Sea Fossils: Fossils of ancient marine life can be found in the Flinders Ranges, indicating the region was once covered by an inland sea.

Kangaroo Island: This island is known for its stunning landscapes and is home to unique wildlife, including sea lions and little penguins.

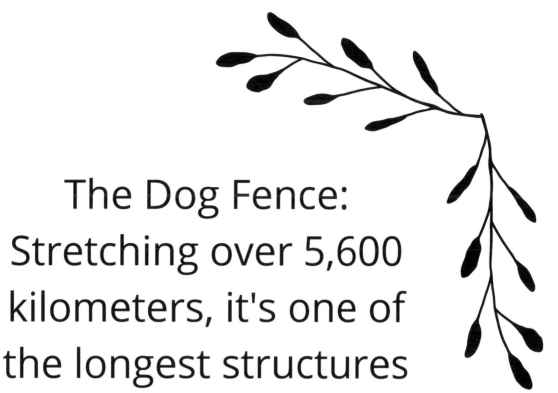

The Dog Fence:
Stretching over 5,600
kilometers, it's one of
the longest structures
in the world and built
to keep dingoes away
from fertile lands.

Rabbit-Proof Fence:
Built to keep rabbits
from spreading, it's
one of the world's
longest fences.

Sydney's Blue Mountains: The blue haze comes from the release of volatile oils from eucalyptus trees.

Wild Camel
Population: Australia
has one of the world's
largest populations of
wild camels.

The Biggest Country Without Borders: Australia is the largest country without any land borders, entirely surrounded by water.

Dolphin-Feeding Tradition: At Tin Can Bay, locals have been feeding wild Indo-Pacific humpback dolphins for generations.

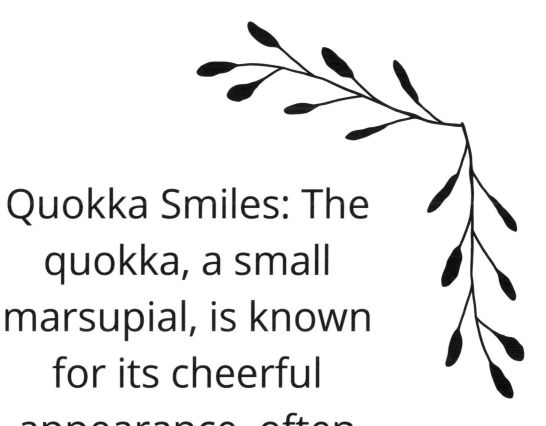

Quokka Smiles: The quokka, a small marsupial, is known for its cheerful appearance, often described as the "world's happiest animal."

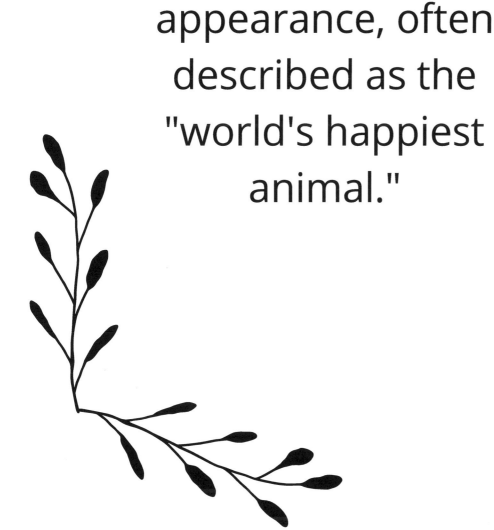

The Pink Galah: Australia is home to the pink and grey galah, a highly intelligent and social parrot.

Goulburn's Big Merino: A giant concrete merino in Goulburn, New South Wales, stands as a tribute to the local wool industry.

The Stockwhip: The stockwhip, a traditional Australian whip, is used by stockmen and women for herding livestock.

Wine Capital: Australia is one of the world's top wine producers, with famous regions like the Barossa Valley and Margaret River.

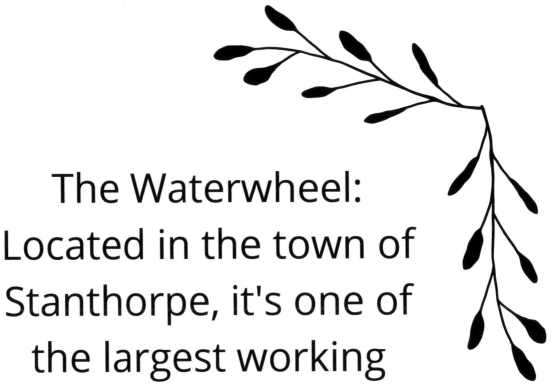

The Waterwheel:
Located in the town of
Stanthorpe, it's one of
the largest working
waterwheels in the
Southern
Hemisphere.

The Giant Earthworm: Gippsland, Victoria, is home to the giant Gippsland earthworm, which can grow up to three feet long.

The Dog Cemetery: In Queensland's Queensland's Daintree Rainforest, there's a pet cemetery with memorials for beloved animals.

The Crooked Hotel: In Nambour, Queensland, there's a pub built from 247 doors.

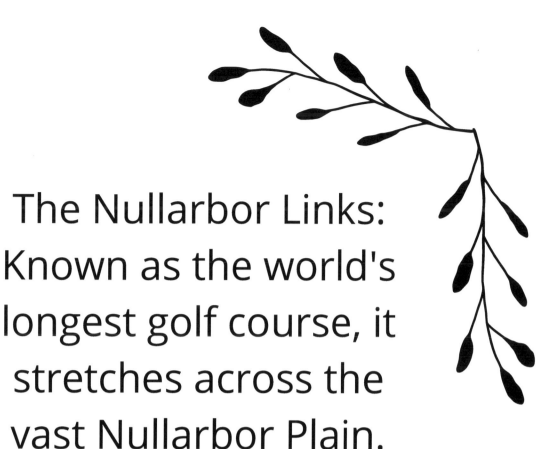

The Nullarbor Links:
Known as the world's
longest golf course, it
stretches across the
vast Nullarbor Plain.

Gold Rush Town: Ballarat in Victoria was a significant site during the Australian gold rush in the 1850s and home to the famous "Eureka Stockade" rebellion.

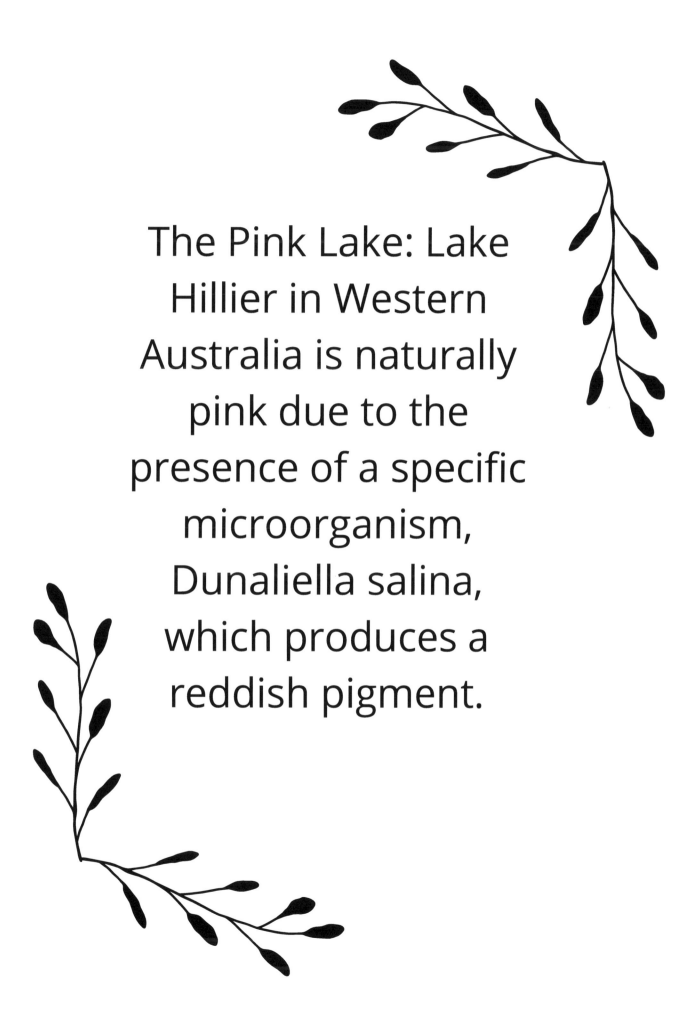

The Pink Lake: Lake Hillier in Western Australia is naturally pink due to the presence of a specific microorganism, Dunaliella salina, which produces a reddish pigment.

Indigenous Dot Art:
Indigenous Australian
art often features "dot
painting," a technique
where small dots are
meticulously applied
to create intricate and
colorful designs.

Barramundi Fishing: The barramundi is a popular sport fish in Australia, prized for its size, strength, and delicious flesh.

Boomerang History:
Boomerangs were
initially used as
hunting tools by
Indigenous
Australians and come
in various shapes and
sizes, each with its
own purpose.

Boomerang History:
Boomerangs were
initially used as
hunting tools by
Indigenous
Australians and come
in various shapes and
sizes, each with its
own purpose.

Thank You
for Exploring Australia

As we reach the end of our journey through "100 Facts About Australia," we hope you've enjoyed this exploration of the Land Down Under as much as we have. Australia is a land of boundless beauty, unique wonders, and vibrant culture, and we've only scratched the surface.

We encourage you to continue your own adventures, whether it's planning a visit to Australia, delving deeper into its history, or simply sharing the stories and facts you've discovered with friends and family.

Australia, with its rugged outback, stunning coastlines, and dynamic cities, will forever hold a special place in our hearts. It's a land of unique animals, ancient cultures, and breathtaking landscapes. We're grateful for the opportunity to share these 100 facts with you.

We invite you to explore the world around you, to seek knowledge, and to embrace the wonders of our planet. There is so much more to discover, so many stories left untold. May your thirst for knowledge and adventure never cease.

Thank you for being a part of this journey. Safe travels, and may your future explorations be filled with wonder and discovery.

Made in the USA
Las Vegas, NV
20 December 2023

83303689R00074